Cram101 Textbook Outlines to accompany:

Human Resource Management for the Hospitality and Tourism Industries

Dennis Nickson, 1st Edition

A Content Technologies Inc. publication (c) 2011.

craml0l.com

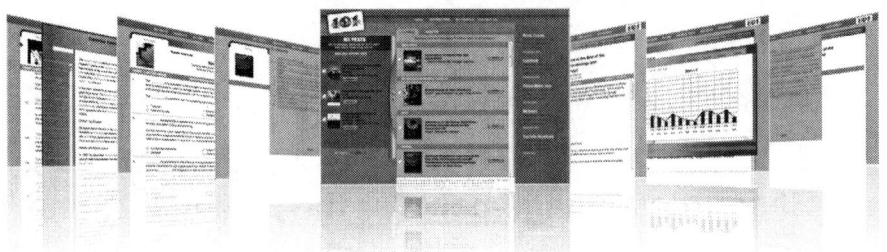

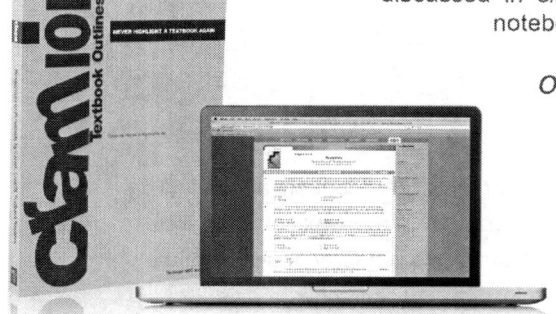

Learning System

Cram101 Textbook Outlines is a learning system. The notes in this book are the highlights of your textbook, you will never have to highlight a book again.

How to use this book. Take this book to class, it is your notebook for the lecture. The notes and highlights on the left hand side of the pages follow the outline and order of the textbook. All you have to do is follow along while your instructor presents the lecture. Circle the items emphasized in class and add other important information on the right side. With Cram101 Textbook Outlines you'll spend less time writing and more time listening. Learning becomes more efficient.

Cram101.com Online

Increase your studying efficiency by using Cram101.com's practice tests and online reference material. It is the perfect complement to Cram101 Textbook Outlines. Use self-teaching matching tests or simulate in-class testing with comprehensive multiple choice tests, or simply use Cram's true and false tests for quick review. Cram101.com even allows you to enter your in-class notes for an integrated studying format combining the textbook notes with your class notes.

Visit **www.Cram101.com**, click Sign Up at the top of the screen, and enter **DK73DW12733** in the promo code box on the registration screen. Your access to www.Cram101.com is discounted by 50% because you have purchased this book. Sign up and stop highlighting textbooks forever.

Human Resource Management for the Hospitality and Tourism Industries
Dennis Nickson, 1st

CONTENTS

Chapter 1. Human resource management and the tourism Chapter 0 and hospitality industry

Skill	A Skill is the learned capacity to carry out pre-determined results often with the minimum outlay of time, energy, or both. Skills can often be divided into domain-general and domain-specific Skills. For example, in the domain of work, some general Skills would include time management, teamwork and leadership, self motivation and others, whereas domain-specific Skills would be useful only for a certain job.
Organization	An Organization is a social arrangement which pursues collective goals, controls its own performance, and has a boundary separating it from its environment. The word itself is derived from the Greek word organon, itself derived from the better-known word ergon.
	In the social sciences, Organizations are the object of analysis for a number of disciplines, such as sociology, economics, political science, psychology, management, and Organizational communication.
Competitive advantage	Competitive advantage is a position of a company in a competitive landscape that allows the company earning return on investments higher than the cost of investments. Competitive advantage should be relevant, unique, and sustainable.
	Competitive advantage is a theory that seeks to address some of the criticisms of comparative advantage.
Best practice	A Best practice is a technique, method, process, activity, incentive, or reward that is believed to be more effective at delivering a particular outcome than any other technique, method, process, etc. when applied to a particular condition or circumstance. The idea is that with proper processes, checks, and testing, a desired outcome can be delivered with fewer problems and unforeseen complications.
Role	A Role or a social Role is a set of connected behaviors, rights and obligations as conceptualized by actors in a social situation. It is an expected or free or continuously changing behavior and may have a given individual social status or social position. It is vital to both functionalist and interactionist understandings of society. Social Role posits the following about social behavior:
	· The division of labor in society takes the form of the interaction among heterogeneous specialized positions, we call Roles.
	· Social Roles included appropriate and permitted forms of behavior, guided by social norms, which are commonly known and hence determine the expectations for appropriate behavior in these Roles.

· Roles are occupied by individuals, who are called actors.

· When individuals approve of a social Role they will incur costs to conform to Role norms, and will also incur costs to punish those who violate Role norms.

· Changed conditions can render a social Role outdated or illegitimate, in which case social pressures are likely to lead to Role change

· The anticipation of rewards and punishments, as well as the satisfaction of behaving prosocially, account for why agents conform to Role requirements.

Strategy	A strategy is a plan of action designed to achieve a particular goal. The word strategy has military connotations, because it derives from the Greek word for army. strategy is different from tactics.
Job security	Job security is the probability that an individual will keep his or her job; a job with a high level of Job security is such that a person with the job would have a small chance of becoming unemployed. Job security is dependent on economy, prevailing business conditions, and the individual`s personal skills. It has been found that people have more Job security in times of economic expansion and less in times of a recession.
Recruitment	Recruitment refers to the process of attracting, screening, and selecting qualified people for a job at an organization or firm. For some components of the Recruitment process, mid- and large-size organizations often retain professional recruiters or outsource some of the process to Recruitment agencies. The Recruitment industry has five main types of agencies: employment agencies, Recruitment websites and job search engines, `headhunters` for executive and professional Recruitment, niche agencies which specialize in a particular area of staffing and in-house Recruitment.
Teamwork	Teamwork is a joint action by two or more people or a group, in which each person contributes with different skills and Express his or her individual interests and opinions to the unity and efficiency of the group in order to achieve common goals.

This does not mean that the individual is no longer important; however, it does mean that effective and efficient teamwork goes beyond individual accomplishments. The most effective teamwork is produced when all the individuals involved harmonize their contributions and work towards a common goal.

Training and development

In the field of human resource management, Training and development is the field concerned with organizational activity aimed at bettering the performance of individuals and groups in organizational settings. It has been known by several names, including employee development, human resource development, and learning and development.

Harrison observes that the name was endlessly debated by the Chartered Institute of Personnel and Development during its review of professional standards in 1999/2000. `Employee Development` was seen as too evocative of the master-slave relationship between employer and employee for those who refer to their employees as `partners` or `associates` to be comfortable with.

Enhancer

In genetics, an enhancer is a short region of DNA that can be bound with proteins (namely, the trans-acting factors, much like a set of transcription factors) to enhance transcription levels of genes (hence the name) in a gene cluster. Furthermore, an enhancer is a cis-acting DNA sequence(s) which can increase transcription of genes. An enhancer does not need to be particularly close to the genes it acts on, and need not be located on the same chromosome.

Chapter 2. International human resource management

Human resource	The objective of Human resources development is to foster Human resourcefulness through enlightened and cohesive policies in education, training, health and employment at all levels, from corporate to national.
Corporate culture	Corporate culture is the total sum of the values, customs, traditions and meanings that make a company unique. Corporate culture is often called `the character of an organization` since it embodies the vision of the company`s founders. The values of a Corporate culture influence the ethical standards within a corporation, as well as managerial behavior.
Role	A Role or a social Role is a set of connected behaviors, rights and obligations as conceptualized by actors in a social situation. It is an expected or free or continuously changing behavior and may have a given individual social status or social position. It is vital to both functionalist and interactionist understandings of society. Social Role posits the following about social behavior:

· The division of labor in society takes the form of the interaction among heterogeneous specialized positions, we call Roles.

· Social Roles included appropriate and permitted forms of behavior, guided by social norms, which are commonly known and hence determine the expectations for appropriate behavior in these Roles.

· Roles are occupied by individuals, who are called actors.

· When individuals approve of a social Role they will incur costs to conform to Role norms, and will also incur costs to punish those who violate Role norms.

· Changed conditions can render a social Role outdated or illegitimate, in which case social pressures are likely to lead to Role change

· The anticipation of rewards and punishments, as well as the satisfaction of behaving prosocially, account for why agents conform to Role requirements.

| Value | A personal and cultural value is a relative ethic value, an assumption upon which implementation can be extrapolated. A value system is a set of consistent values and measures that are not true. A principle value is a foundation upon which other values and measures of integrity are based. |

Chapter 3. Organizational culture

Organizational culture	Organizational culture is an idea in the field of Organizational studies and management which describes the psychology, attitudes, experiences, beliefs and values (personal and cultural values) of an organization. It has been defined as `the specific collection of values and norms that are shared by people and groups in an organization and that control the way they interact with each other and with stakeholders outside the organization.` This definition continues to explain organizational values, also known as `beliefs and ideas about what kinds of goals members of an organization should pursue and ideas about the appropriate kinds or standards of behavior organizational members should use to achieve these goals. From organizational values develop organizational norms, guidelines, or expectations that prescribe appropriate kinds of behavior by employees in particular situations and control the behavior of organizational members towards one another.` Organizational culture is not the same as corporate culture.
Corporate culture	Corporate culture is the total sum of the values, customs, traditions and meanings that make a company unique. Corporate culture is often called `the character of an organization` since it embodies the vision of the company`s founders. The values of a Corporate culture influence the ethical standards within a corporation, as well as managerial behavior.
Corporate architecture	Corporate architecture is an architectonic discipline which focuses on designing and constructing buildings, spaces or environments with the aim of meeting the needs of a business community (a corporation).
Mission statement	A mission statement is a formal short written statement of the purpose of a company or organization. The mission statement should guide the actions of the organization, spell out its overall goal, provide a sense of direction, and guide decision-making. It provides `the framework or context within which the companyÂ´s strategies are formulated.` Historically it is associated with Christian religious groups; indeed, for many years a missionary was assumed to be a person on a specifically religious mission.
Value	A personal and cultural value is a relative ethic value, an assumption upon which implementation can be extrapolated. A value system is a set of consistent values and measures that are not true. A principle value is a foundation upon which other values and measures of integrity are based.

Chapter 3. Organizational culture

Organization	An Organization is a social arrangement which pursues collective goals, controls its own performance, and has a boundary separating it from its environment. The word itself is derived from the Greek word organon, itself derived from the better-known word ergon.
	In the social sciences, Organizations are the object of analysis for a number of disciplines, such as sociology, economics, political science, psychology, management, and Organizational communication.
Aesthetic	Aesthetics (also spelled æsthetics or esthetics) is commonly known as the study of sensory or sensori-emotional values scholars in the field define aesthetics as `critical reflection on art, culture and nature.` aesthetics is a subdiscipline of axiology, a branch of philosophy, and is closely associated with the philosophy of art. aesthetics studies new ways of seeing and of perceiving the world.
Corporate identity	In marketing, a Corporate identity is the `persona` of a corporation which is designed to accord with and facilitate the attainment of business objectives. It is usually visibly manifested by way of branding and the use of trademarks.
	Corporate identity comes into being when there is a common ownership of an organizational philosophy that is manifest in a distinct corporate culture -- the corporate personality.
Style guide	A style guide or style manual is a set of standards for design and writing of documents, either for general use or for a specific publication or organization. style guides are prevalent for general and specialized use, for the general reading and writing audience, and for students and scholars of the various academic disciplines, medicine, journalism, the law, government, business, and industry. Some style guides focus on graphic design, covering such topics as typography and white space.

Chapter 4. Labour markets

Supply of labor	In mainstream economic theories, the supply of labor is the number of total hours that workers wish to work at a given real wage rate. Realistically, the labor supply is a function of various factors within an economy. For instance, overpopulation increases the number of available workers driving down wages and can result in high unemployment.
Skill	A Skill is the learned capacity to carry out pre-determined results often with the minimum outlay of time, energy, or both. Skills can often be divided into domain-general and domain-specific Skills. For example, in the domain of work, some general Skills would include time management, teamwork and leadership, self motivation and others, whereas domain-specific Skills would be useful only for a certain job.
Ethical bank	An Ethical bank is a bank concerned with the social and environmental impacts of its investments and loans. Ethical banks are part of a larger societal movement toward more social and environmental responsibility in the financial sector. This movement includes: ethical investment, socially responsible investment, corporate social responsibility, and is also related to such movements as the fair trade movement, ethical consumerism, boycotting, etc.
Employment	Employment is a contract between two parties, one being the employer and the other being the employee. An employee may be defined as: `A person in the service of another under any contract of hire, express or implied, oral or written, where the employer has the power or right to control and direct the employee in the material details of how the work is to be performed.` Black`s Law Dictionary page 471 (5th ed. 1979).
	In a commercial setting, the employer conceives of a productive activity, generally with the intention of generating a profit, and the employee contributes labour to the enterprise, usually in return for payment of wages.
Parental Leave	Parental leave is an employee benefit that provides paid or unpaid time off work to care for a child or make arrangements for the child`s welfare. Often, the term Parental leave includes maternity, paternity, and adoption leave. Often the minimum benefits are stipulated by law.
Right	Rights are normative (e.g. legal, social, or ethical) principles of freedom or entitlement. That is to say, Rights are rules about what is allowed of people or owed to people, according to some legal system, social convention, or ethical theory. The concept of Rights is often fundamental to civilized societies, and it is of vital importance in such disciplines as law and ethics, especially theories of justice and deontology.

Chapter 4. Labour markets

Trade Union	A Trade union or labor union is an organization of workers who have banded together to achieve common goals such as better working conditions. The Trade union, through its leadership, bargains with the employer on behalf of union members (rank and file members) and negotiates labour contracts (collective bargaining) with employers. This may include the negotiation of wages, work rules, complaint procedures, rules governing hiring, firing and promotion of workers, benefits, workplace safety and policies.
Wage	A Wage is a compensation, usually financial, received by workers in exchange for their labor. Compensation in terms of Wages is given to workers and compensation in terms of salary is given to employees. Compensation is a monetary benefit given to employees in return for the services provided by them.
Employee Relations Act 1999	The Employee Relations Act 1999 is a British law. The Act allows workers to receive at least 3 months unpaid leave for the purpose of caring for a child. Mothers can have up to 18 weeks paid maternity leave.
Extreme value	The largest and the smallest element of a set are called extreme values, absolute extrema, extreme records, or optima. For a differentiable function f, if $f(x_0)$ is an extreme value for the set of all values $f(x)$, and if x_0 is in the interior of the domain of f, then x_0 is a critical point, by Fermat`s theorem. The point or points at which a function assumes its maximum (respectively, minimum) value are called the arg max (respectively, arg min): the arguments (inputs) at which the maximum (respectively, minimum) occurs.
Minimum Wage	A Minimum wage is the lowest hourly, daily or monthly wage that employers may legally pay to employees or workers. Equivalently, it is the lowest wage at which workers may sell their labor. Although Minimum wage laws are in effect in a great many jurisdictions, there are differences of opinion about the benefits and drawbacks of a Minimum wage.
Part-time	A Part-time job is a form of employment that carries fewer hours per week than a full-time job. Workers are considered to be Part-time if they commonly work fewer than 30 or 35 hours per week. According to the International Labour Organization, the number of Part-time workers has increased from one-fourth to a half in the past 20 years in most developed countries, excluding the United States.

Chapter 4. Labour markets

Regulations	The Control of Substances Hazardous to Health regulations 2002 is a United Kingdom Statutory Instrument that stipulates general requirements on employers to protect employees and other persons from the hazards of substances used at work by risk assessment, control of exposure, health surveillance and incident planning. There are also duties on employees to take care of their own exposure to hazardous substances and prohibitions on the import of certain substances into the European Economic Area. The regulations reenacted with amendements the Control of Substances Hazardous to Work regulations 1999 and implement several European Union directives.
Utilization	Utilization is a statistical concept (Queueing Theory) as well as a primary business measure for the rental industry. In queueing theory, utilization is the proportion of the system`s resources which is used by the traffic which arrives at it. It should be strictly less than one for the system to function well.
Peripheral	A peripheral is a device attached to a host computer but not part of it whose primary functionality is dependent upon the host, and can therefore be considered as expanding the host`s capabilities, while not forming part of the system`s core architecture. Examples are printers, scanners, tape drives, microphones, speakers, webcams, and cameras. Whether something is a peripheral or part of a computer is not always clearly demarcated; a video capture card inside a computer case is not part of the core computer but is contained in the case.
Cross-training	Cross-training refers to training in different ways to improve overall performance. It takes advantage of the particular effectiveness of each training method, while at the same time attempting to neglect the shortcomings of that method by combining it with other methods that address its weaknesses. With respect to employee-employer relationship, Cross-training refers to the training of one employee to do another`s work.

Chapter 5. Recruitment and selection

Skill	A Skill is the learned capacity to carry out pre-determined results often with the minimum outlay of time, energy, or both. Skills can often be divided into domain-general and domain-specific Skills. For example, in the domain of work, some general Skills would include time management, teamwork and leadership, self motivation and others, whereas domain-specific Skills would be useful only for a certain job.
Job analysis	Job analysis refers to various methodologies for analyzing the requirements of a job. The main purpose of conducting Job analysis is to prepare job description and job specification which in turn helps to hire the right quality of workforce into the organization. The general purpose of Job analysis is to document the requirements of a job and the work performed.
Recruitment	Recruitment refers to the process of attracting, screening, and selecting qualified people for a job at an organization or firm. For some components of the Recruitment process, mid- and large-size organizations often retain professional recruiters or outsource some of the process to Recruitment agencies.
	The Recruitment industry has five main types of agencies: employment agencies, Recruitment websites and job search engines, `headhunters` for executive and professional Recruitment, niche agencies which specialize in a particular area of staffing and in-house Recruitment.
Job description	A Job description is a list of the general tasks, or functions, and responsibilities of a position. Typically, it also includes to whom the position reports, specifications such as the qualifications needed by the person in the job, salary range for the position, etc. A Job description is usually developed by conducting a job analysis, which includes examining the tasks and sequences of tasks necessary to perform the job.
Aesthetic	Aesthetics (also spelled æsthetics or esthetics) is commonly known as the study of sensory or sensori-emotional values scholars in the field define aesthetics as `critical reflection on art, culture and nature.` aesthetics is a subdiscipline of axiology, a branch of philosophy, and is closely associated with the philosophy of art. aesthetics studies new ways of seeing and of perceiving the world.
Interpersonal skills	Interpersonal skills are the skills that a person uses to interact with other people. Interpersonal skills are sometimes also referred to as people skills or communication skills. Interpersonal skills involve using skills such as active listening and tone of voice, they include delegation and leadership.

Chapter 5. Recruitment and selection

Ethical bank	An Ethical bank is a bank concerned with the social and environmental impacts of its investments and loans. Ethical banks are part of a larger societal movement toward more social and environmental responsibility in the financial sector. This movement includes: ethical investment, socially responsible investment, corporate social responsibility, and is also related to such movements as the fair trade movement, ethical consumerism, boycotting, etc.
Social skill	A Social skill is any skill facilitating interaction and communication with others. Social rules and relations are created, communicated, and changed in verbal and nonverbal ways. The process of learning such skills is called socialization.
Strategy	A strategy is a plan of action designed to achieve a particular goal. The word strategy has military connotations, because it derives from the Greek word for army. strategy is different from tactics.
Chartered Institute of Personnel and Development	The Chartered Institute of Personnel and Development (CIPD) is Europe`s largest professional institute for people management and development. It is located in Wimbledon, London, England. The organisation has over 133,000 members, and achieved chartered status in 2000. The institute holds an annual conference for HR practitioners.  · 1913 to 1917: Welfare Workers` Association (WWA) · 1917 to 1924: Central Association of Welfare Workers (CAWW), Central Association of Welfare Workers (Industrial), Welfare Workers` Institute (WWI) · 1924 to 1931: Institute of Industrial Welfare Workers (IIWW) · 1931 to 1946: Institute of Labour Management (ILM) · 1946 to 1994: Institute of Personnel Management (IPM) · 1994 to 2000: Institute of Personnel and Development (IPD)- an amalgamation of the IPM and Institute of Training and Development (ITD) - (formerly Institute of Training Officers) · 2000 to present: Chartered Institute of Personnel and Development (CIPD) Chartered status was achieved in 2000 and the CIPD came into existence from 1 July of that year

· CIPD professional qualifications

· Professional Assessment of Competence (PAC)

· Accreditation of Prior Certificated Learning (APCL)

· Affiliate membership

· Affiliate: a basic level of membership, not assessed against professional standards.

· Associate: awarded on completion of a support level certificate or relevant NVQ Level 3 and 4.

· Licentiate: awarded on completion of at least one of the first three fields of the Practitioner-level professional standards, and also on completion of relevant MBAs and NVQs (Level 5).

· Graduate: awarded on completion of all fields of the Practitioner-level professional standards, but where no significant HR experience is held.

· Chartered Member (Chartered MCIPD)
Awarded on request to graduate members with have three years` relevant managerial experience.

Recruitment advertising	Recruitment advertising includes all communications used by an organization to attract talent to work within it. Recruitment advertisements may be the first impression of a company for many people, and the first impression the firm makes goes a long way to determining interest in the job opening being advertised. Recruitment advertisements typically have a uniform layout and contain the following elements: · the job title heading and location · an explanatory paragraph describing the company, including the Employer Brand

· a description of the position

· entry qualifications

· the remuneration package

· further details and from where application forms may be sought

In the United Kingdom many recruitment advertisements fail to provide all the information listed above and this is frustrating for potential applicants.

When faced with hiring many roles, corporate employers have many channels and options to choose from. They may:

· A retained search firm

· A contingency search firm

· Retain a recruitment process outsourcing organization

· Use a candidate fulfillment service

· Retain a Recruitment advertising agency

· Retain a specialist interactive Recruitment advertising agency

· Leverage old media to advertise their openings (print, radio and television)

· Leverage job boards

· Leverage new media

· Invest in additional internal resources

	Each of these channels has its benefits and many firms will use a mix of some or all of the above options.
GROW model	The GROW model (or process) is a technique for problem solving or goal setting. It was developed in the UK and used extensively in the corporate coaching market in the late 1980s and 1990s. There have been many claims to authorship of GROW as a way of achieving goals and solving problems.
Recruitment process	`Onboarding` is a term which describes the introduction or `induction` process. A well-planned introduction helps new employees become fully operational quickly and is often integrated with a new company and environment. Onboarding is included in the recruitment process for retention purposes.
Assessment	Educational Assessment is the process of documenting, usually in measurable terms, knowledge, skills, attitudes and beliefs. Assessment can focus on the individual learner, the learning community (class, workshop, or other organized group of learners), the institution, or the educational system as a whole. According to the Academic Exchange Quarterly: `Studies of a theoretical or empirical nature (including case studies, portfolio studies, exploratory, or experimental work) addressing the Assessment of learner aptitude and preparation, motivation and learning styles, learning outcomes in achievement and satisfaction in different educational contexts are all welcome, as are studies addressing issues of measurable standards and benchmarks`.
Selection criteria	This is used by Government bodies and Not for Profit Organisations to aid the hiring of employees.
	STAR: Situation, Task, Actions ' Results.
	This model helps to construct sentences to meet the set Selection criteria.
	· Situation - Set the context by describing the circumstance where you used the skills or qualities and gained the experience
	· Task - What was your role is completing this task
	· Actions - What you did and how you did it

· Results - What did you achieved.

Interaction	Interaction is a kind of action that occurs as two or more objects have an effect upon one another. The idea of a two-way effect is essential in the concept of Interaction, as opposed to a one-way causal effect. A closely related term is interconnectivity, which deals with the Interactions of Interactions within systems: combinations of many simple Interactions can lead to surprising emergent phenomena.
Two-way	Two-way communication occurs when information flows in both directions between two parties. In journalism, a two-way is an informal style of reporting that involves a conversation between two people. The most common arrangement is for a reporter in the field to talk to the host of a news program.
Personality test	A Personality test aims to describe aspects of a person`s character that remain stable throughout that person`s lifetime, the individual`s character pattern of behavior, thoughts, and feelings. An early model of personality was posited by Greek philosopher/physician Hippocrates. The 20th century heralded a new interest in defining and identifying separate personality types, in close correlation with the emergence of the field of psychology.
Commission	The Health and Safety Commission (HSC), was a United Kingdom non-departmental public body. The HSC was created by the Health and Safety at Work etc. Act 1974 (HSWA).
Commission for Racial Equality	The Commission for Racial Equality (CRE) was a non-departmental public body in the United Kingdom which aimed to tackle racial discrimination and promote racial equality. Its work has been merged into the new Equality and Human Rights Commission, though it will subsist as a separate body until 2009. The commission was established by the Race Relations Act 1976, passed by James Callaghan`s Labour government. The first director of the commission was former Conservative M.P., David Lane.
Equal	EQUAL was the `Community Initiative` within the European Social Fund of the European Union. It concerned `transnational co-operation to promote new means of combating all forms of discrimination and inEQUALities in connection with the labour market`. It ran from 2001 till 2007 with a budget of some â,¬3 billion of EU resources, matched by a similar sum from national resources.
Equality of opportunity	Equality of opportunity is a term which has differing definitions and there is no consensus as to the precise meaning. In the classical sense, Equality of opportunity is closely aligned with the concept of equality before the law, and ideas of meritocracy.

Chapter 5. Recruitment and selection

Equality of opportunity is in philosophical contrast to the concept of equality of outcome.

Equal Opportunities Commission	The Equal Opportunities Commission was an independent non-departmental public body, (NDPB) in the United Kingdom, which tackled sex discrimination and promoted gender equality. It was set up under the Sex Discrimination Act 1975 and had statutory powers to help enforce this Act, the Equal Pay Act and other gender equality legislation that existed in Britain. Due to the ability of the Scottish Parliament and Welsh Assembly to vary the law in this area, separate Equal Opportunities Commission sub-agencies existed for Scotland and Wales.
Content validity	In psychometrics, Content validity refers to the extent to which a measure represents all facets of a given social construct. For example, a depression scale may lack Content validity if it only assesses the affective dimension of depression but fails to take into account the behavioral dimension. An element of subjectivity exists in relation to determining Content validity, which requires a degree of agreement about what a particular personality trait such as extraversion represents.
Face validity	Face validity is a property of a test intended to measure something. The test is said to have Face validity if it `looks like` it is going to measure what it is supposed to measure. For instance, if you prepare a test to measure whether students can perform multiplication, and the people you show it to all agree that it looks like a good test of multiplication ability, you have shown the Face validity of your test.
Predictive validity	In psychometrics, Predictive validity is the extent to which a score on a scale or test predicts scores on some criterion measure. For example, the validity of a cognitive test for job performance is the correlation between test scores and, for example, supervisor performance ratings. Such a cognitive test would have Predictive validity if the observed correlation were statistically significant.

Clam101

Chapter 6. Equal opportunities and managing diversity

Equal	EQUAL was the `Community Initiative` within the European Social Fund of the European Union. It concerned `transnational co-operation to promote new means of combating all forms of discrimination and inEQUALities in connection with the labour market`. It ran from 2001 till 2007 with a budget of some â,¬3 billion of EU resources, matched by a similar sum from national resources.
Equality of opportunity	Equality of opportunity is a term which has differing definitions and there is no consensus as to the precise meaning. In the classical sense, Equality of opportunity is closely aligned with the concept of equality before the law, and ideas of meritocracy. Equality of opportunity is in philosophical contrast to the concept of equality of outcome.
Employment	Employment is a contract between two parties, one being the employer and the other being the employee. An employee may be defined as: `A person in the service of another under any contract of hire, express or implied, oral or written, where the employer has the power or right to control and direct the employee in the material details of how the work is to be performed.` Black`s Law Dictionary page 471 (5th ed. 1979). In a commercial setting, the employer conceives of a productive activity, generally with the intention of generating a profit, and the employee contributes labour to the enterprise, usually in return for payment of wages.
Employment tribunal	Employment Tribunals are tribunal non-departmental public bodies in England and Wales and Scotland which have statutory jurisdiction to hear many kinds of disputes between employers and employees. The most common disputes are concerned with unfair dismissal, redundancy payments and employment discrimination. The Tribunals are part of the UK tribunals system, administered by the Tribunals Service and regulated and supervised by the Administrative Justice and Tribunals Council.
Women	A woman (irregular plural: women) is a female human. The term woman is usually reserved for an adult, with the term girl being the usual term for a female child or adolescent. However, the term woman is also sometimes used to identify a female human, regardless of age, as in phrases such as `women`s rights`.
Race Relations Act	The Race Relations Act 1976 was established by the Parliament of the United Kingdom to prevent discrimination on the grounds of race. Items that are covered include discrimination on the grounds of race, colour, nationality, ethnic and national origin in the fields of employment, the provision of goods and services, education and public functions.

	The Act also established the Commission for Racial Equality with a view to review the legislation.
Disability Discrimination Act	In the late 20th and early 21st centuries, a number of countries have passed laws aimed at reducing discrimination against people with disabilities. These laws have begun to appear as the notion of civil rights has become more influential globally, and follow other forms of anti-discrimination and equal opportunity legislation aimed at preventing racial discrimination and sexism which began to emerge in the second half of the 20th century. Australia Disability Discrimination Act 1992 Canada Ontarians with Disabilities Act (2002) (only in Ontario, no other province has disability protection) United Kingdom Disability Discrimination Act 1995 (which has been extended and amended by a number of enactments including the Special Educational Needs and Disability Act 2001 , and the Disability Discrimination Act 2005) United States of America Americans with Disabilities Act of 1990 Pakistan National Policy for Persons with Disablilities 2002 .
Disability Discrimination Act 1995	The Disability Discrimination Act 1995 is an Act of the Parliament of the United Kingdom which makes it unlawful to discriminate against people in respect of their disabilities in relation to employment, the provision of goods and services, education and transport. It is a civil rights law. Other countries use constitutional, social rights or criminal law to make similar provisions.
Human Rights	Human rights are `basic rights and freedoms to which all humans are entitled.` Examples of rights and freedoms which have come to be commonly thought of as Human rights include civil and political rights, such as the right to life and liberty, freedom of expression, and equality before the law; and economic, social and cultural rights, including the right to participate in culture, the right to food, the right to work, and the right to education.

Chapter 6. Equal opportunities and managing diversity

Although other civilizations - notably those of Persia, India, China and the Islamic world - were at least equal to Europe at various stages in history, and in many respects in advance of it, they did not manage to propagate a universal ethics of rights. In the 16th century, the `Great Moghul,` Akbar the Great of India, granted religious minorities legal status in his realm and condemned traditional Indian practices such as the burning of widows (suttee) and slavery.

Human Rights Act

A Human Rights Act is a piece of legislation that sets out individual rights and freedoms under law. Many countries have similar rights enshrined into law; the countries with this naming convention tend to be Commonwealth countries. For specific variations see the articles for relevant act in the following countries:

Australia

The ACT Human Rights Act 2004
The Victorian Charter of Human Rights and Responsibilities Act 2006

Canada

The Canadian Human Rights Act

New Zealand

The Human Rights Act 1993

United Kingdom

The Human Rights Act 1998

.

Chapter 6. Equal opportunities and managing diversity

Human Rights Act 1998	The Human Rights Act 1998 is an Act of Parliament of the United Kingdom which received Royal Assent on 9 November 1998, and mostly came into force on 2 October 2000. Its aim is to `give further effect` in UK law to the rights contained in the European Convention on Human Rights. The Act makes available in UK courts a remedy for breach of a Convention right, without the need to go to the European Court of Human Rights in Strasbourg. It also totally abolished the death penalty in UK law (although this was not required by the Convention in force for the UK at that time).
Regulations	The Control of Substances Hazardous to Health regulations 2002 is a United Kingdom Statutory Instrument that stipulates general requirements on employers to protect employees and other persons from the hazards of substances used at work by risk assessment, control of exposure, health surveillance and incident planning. There are also duties on employees to take care of their own exposure to hazardous substances and prohibitions on the import of certain substances into the European Economic Area. The regulations reenacted with amendements the Control of Substances Hazardous to Work regulations 1999 and implement several European Union directives.
Right	Rights are normative (e.g. legal, social, or ethical) principles of freedom or entitlement. That is to say, Rights are rules about what is allowed of people or owed to people, according to some legal system, social convention, or ethical theory. The concept of Rights is often fundamental to civilized societies, and it is of vital importance in such disciplines as law and ethics, especially theories of justice and deontology.
Commission	The Health and Safety Commission (HSC), was a United Kingdom non-departmental public body. The HSC was created by the Health and Safety at Work etc. Act 1974 (HSWA).
Commission for Racial Equality	The Commission for Racial Equality (CRE) was a non-departmental public body in the United Kingdom which aimed to tackle racial discrimination and promote racial equality. Its work has been merged into the new Equality and Human Rights Commission, though it will subsist as a separate body until 2009. The commission was established by the Race Relations Act 1976, passed by James Callaghan`s Labour government. The first director of the commission was former Conservative M.P., David Lane.
Equal Opportunities Commission	The Equal Opportunities Commission was an independent non-departmental public body, (NDPB) in the United Kingdom, which tackled sex discrimination and promoted gender equality. It was set up under the Sex Discrimination Act 1975 and had statutory powers to help enforce this Act, the Equal Pay Act and other gender equality legislation that existed in Britain. Due to the ability of the Scottish Parliament and Welsh Assembly to vary the law in this area, separate Equal Opportunities Commission sub-agencies existed for Scotland and Wales.

Chapter 6. Equal opportunities and managing diversity

Sex Discrimination Act	The Sex Discrimination Act 1975 is an Act of the Parliament of the United Kingdom to protect men and women from discrimination on the grounds of sex. The Act is mainly in relation to employment, training, education, harassment, the provision of goods and services, and the disposal of premises. The Gender Recognition Act 2004 and the The Sex Discrimination Act 1975 (Amendment) Regulations 2008 amended parts of this Act to apply to transgender people.
Positive action	Positive action is a term used to connote promotion of an under-represented group in the workplace, educational institutions and positions in society, without prejudicing the criteria of selection by merit. In the United Kingdom Equality Act 2010 ss 157-158, the term is used in the context of employment to allow selection of a candidate from an under-represented group, so long as he or she is no less than equally qualified compared to another potential candidate that is not from the under-represented group
Genuine Occupational Qualifications	In UK employment discrimination law, a Genuine Occupational Qualification exists when the nature of a particular job causes the sex or gender of an applicant to become a reasonable cause for choosing one applicant over another. Genuine Occupational Qualificationss are a special case exception to the Employment (Sex Discrimination) Act 2000, defined in Section 9 of this act. There are nine possible types of reason for claiming a Genuine Occupational Qualifications in advertising a particular job: · Physiology or authenticity (for example, in choosing actors to play a role), · Privacy and decency of people the employee would be dealing with (for example, staff in a care home), · Private household`s integrity (for example, professional carers for an individual, but not normally nannies), · Single-sex accommodation, when it is unreasonable to expect the employer to provide additional accommodation, · Single-sex establishments, for example special prisons and refuges,

· Personal welfare and counselling, when sex is directly relevant to the welfare or counselling provided,

· Jobs in foreign countries with specifically relevant laws or customs,

· When a pair of jobs are advertised specifically for a married couple.

· When the manager of a striptease club seeks strippers.
In each of these, reasons must be specific and absolute, not based on stereotypes or generalised assumptions.

· `Genuine Occupational Qualifications`, A Good Practice Guide for Employers, Department of Trade and Industry, retrieved January 2008.

Affirmative action	Affirmative action refers to policies that take factors including `race, color, religion, sex or national origin` into consideration in order to benefit an underrepresented group, usually as a means to counter the effects of a history of discrimination. The focus of such policies ranges from employment and education to public contracting and health programs. `Affirmative action` is action taken to increase the representation of women and minorities in areas of employment, education, and business from which they have been historically excluded.
Religious discrimination	Religious discrimination is valuing or treating a person or group differently because of what they do or do not believe. A concept like that of `Religious discrimination` is necessary to take into account ambiguities of the term religious persecution. The infamous cases in which people have been executed for beliefs perceived to be heretic are generally recognisable as persecution; Other cases in which adherents of different religions (or denominations) are treated unequally before the law are sometimes difficult to assess.
Chartered Institute of Personnel and Development	The Chartered Institute of Personnel and Development (CIPD) is Europe`s largest professional institute for people management and development. It is located in Wimbledon, London, England. The organisation has over 133,000 members, and achieved chartered status in 2000. The institute holds an annual conference for HR practitioners.    · 1913 to 1917: Welfare Workers` Association (WWA)

· 1917 to 1924: Central Association of Welfare Workers (CAWW), Central Association of Welfare Workers (Industrial), Welfare Workers` Institute (WWI)

· 1924 to 1931: Institute of Industrial Welfare Workers (IIWW)

· 1931 to 1946: Institute of Labour Management (ILM)

· 1946 to 1994: Institute of Personnel Management (IPM)

· 1994 to 2000: Institute of Personnel and Development (IPD)- an amalgamation of the IPM and Institute of Training and Development (ITD) - (formerly Institute of Training Officers)

· 2000 to present: Chartered Institute of Personnel and Development (CIPD)
Chartered status was achieved in 2000 and the CIPD came into existence from 1 July of that year

· CIPD professional qualifications

· Professional Assessment of Competence (PAC)

· Accreditation of Prior Certificated Learning (APCL)

· Affiliate membership

· Affiliate: a basic level of membership, not assessed against professional standards.

· Associate: awarded on completion of a support level certificate or relevant NVQ Level 3 and 4.

· Licentiate: awarded on completion of at least one of the first three fields of the Practitioner-level professional standards, and also on completion of relevant MBAs and NVQs (Level 5).

· Graduate: awarded on completion of all fields of the Practitioner-level professional standards, but where no significant HR experience is held.

· Chartered Member (Chartered MCIPD)
Awarded on request to graduate members with have three years` relevant managerial experience.

Workforce

The Workforce is the labour pool in employment. It is generally used to describe those working for a single company or industry, but can also apply to a geographic region like a city, country, state, etc. The term generally excludes the employers or management, and implies those involved in manual labour.

Management

Management in all business areas and organizational activities are the acts of getting people together to accomplish desired goals and objectives. Management comprises planning, organizing, staffing, leading or directing, and controlling an organization or effort for the purpose of accomplishing a goal. Resourcing encompasses the deployment and manipulation of human resources, financial resources, technological resources, and natural resources.

Organization

An Organization is a social arrangement which pursues collective goals, controls its own performance, and has a boundary separating it from its environment. The word itself is derived from the Greek word organon, itself derived from the better-known word ergon.

In the social sciences, Organizations are the object of analysis for a number of disciplines, such as sociology, economics, political science, psychology, management, and Organizational communication.

Chapter 7. Training and development

Human resource	The objective of Human resources development is to foster Human resourcefulness through enlightened and cohesive policies in education, training, health and employment at all levels, from corporate to national.
Chartered Institute of Personnel and Development	The Chartered Institute of Personnel and Development (CIPD) is Europe`s largest professional institute for people management and development. It is located in Wimbledon, London, England. The organisation has over 133,000 members, and achieved chartered status in 2000. The institute holds an annual conference for HR practitioners.  · 1913 to 1917: Welfare Workers` Association (WWA) · 1917 to 1924: Central Association of Welfare Workers (CAWW), Central Association of Welfare Workers (Industrial), Welfare Workers` Institute (WWI) · 1924 to 1931: Institute of Industrial Welfare Workers (IIWW) · 1931 to 1946: Institute of Labour Management (ILM) · 1946 to 1994: Institute of Personnel Management (IPM) · 1994 to 2000: Institute of Personnel and Development (IPD)- an amalgamation of the IPM and Institute of Training and Development (ITD) - (formerly Institute of Training Officers) · 2000 to present: Chartered Institute of Personnel and Development (CIPD) Chartered status was achieved in 2000 and the CIPD came into existence from 1 July of that year · CIPD professional qualifications · Professional Assessment of Competence (PAC) · Accreditation of Prior Certificated Learning (APCL) · Affiliate membership

· Affiliate: a basic level of membership, not assessed against professional standards.

· Associate: awarded on completion of a support level certificate or relevant NVQ Level 3 and 4.

· Licentiate: awarded on completion of at least one of the first three fields of the Practitioner-level professional standards, and also on completion of relevant MBAs and NVQs (Level 5).

· Graduate: awarded on completion of all fields of the Practitioner-level professional standards, but where no significant HR experience is held.

· Chartered Member (Chartered MCIPD)
Awarded on request to graduate members with have three years` relevant managerial experience.

Job description	A Job description is a list of the general tasks, or functions, and responsibilities of a position. Typically, it also includes to whom the position reports, specifications such as the qualifications needed by the person in the job, salary range for the position, etc. A Job description is usually developed by conducting a job analysis, which includes examining the tasks and sequences of tasks necessary to perform the job.
Apprenticeship	Apprenticeship is a system of training a new generation of practitioners of a skill. Apprentices or protégés build their careers from Apprenticeships. Most of their training is done on the job while working for an employer who helps the apprentices learn their trade, in exchange for their continuing labour for an agreed period after they become skilled.
Skill	A Skill is the learned capacity to carry out pre-determined results often with the minimum outlay of time, energy, or both. Skills can often be divided into domain-general and domain-specific Skills. For example, in the domain of work, some general Skills would include time management, teamwork and leadership, self motivation and others, whereas domain-specific Skills would be useful only for a certain job.
Superhost	Superhost was a character portrayed by TV personality Marty Sullivan at independent television station WUAB-43 in Cleveland from 1969 to 1990. He wore a baggy suit, cape and red nose (like a clown version of Superman) to host the station`s Saturday afternoon monster movie.

The show would begin at noon with an hour called Supe's On, generally an hour-long warm-up to the movies, with a Laurel and Hardy short sandwiched between two Three Stooges shorts. Superhost would appear between these, cracking jokes and talking to the TV audience.

Total quality management

Total quality management is a management concept coined by W. Edwards Deming. The basis of Total quality management is to reduce the errors produced during the manufacturing or service process, increase customer satisfaction, streamline supply chain management, aim for modernization of equipment and ensure workers have the highest level of training. One of the principal aims of Total quality management is to limit errors to 1 per 1 million units produced.

Induction

Induction nduction (educator)
Induction nduction is the support and guidance provided to novice teachers and school administrators in the early stages of their careers. Induction nduction encompasses orientation to the workplace, socialization, mentoring, and guidance through beginning teacher practice.

Comprehensive, high-quality Induction consists of several key elements:

· a multi-year program

· rigorous mentor selection and training

· subject-area pairing of mentors and beginning educators

· sufficient time for mentors to meet with and observe new educators

· formative assessment that assists beginning educators to advance along a continuum of professional growth.
The New Teacher Center Induction model is nationally recognized in the United States for its promotion of new educator development and its impact on teacher retention and student learning.

Mission statement

A mission statement is a formal short written statement of the purpose of a company or organization. The mission statement should guide the actions of the organization, spell out its overall goal, provide a sense of direction, and guide decision-making. It provides `the framework or context within which the companyÂ´s strategies are formulated.`

Historically it is associated with Christian religious groups; indeed, for many years a missionary was assumed to be a person on a specifically religious mission.

Chapter 8. Performance management and performance appraisal

Performance appraisal	A Performance appraisal, employee appraisal, performance review, or (career) development discussion is a method by which the job performance of an employee is evaluated (generally in terms of quality, quantity, cost, and time) typically by the corresponding manager or supervisor. A Performance appraisal is a part of guiding and managing career development. It is the process of obtaining, analyzing, and recording information about the relative worth of an employee to the organization.
Performance management	In the case of business, the typical approach is to create `smart goals,` those which are specific, measurable, achievable, relevant, and timely. This management process can involve self-management (e.g., lone workers using the same tools as found in formal management structures or patient learning to manage self care procedures) or the formal chains of management typically found in most organizations where people work in groups or teams. Management under this performance management definition is about arranging the conditions of the workplace for individual, group, unit, division, regional, and corporate success.
Chartered Institute of Personnel and Development	The Chartered Institute of Personnel and Development (CIPD) is Europe`s largest professional institute for people management and development. It is located in Wimbledon, London, England. The organisation has over 133,000 members, and achieved chartered status in 2000. The institute holds an annual conference for HR practitioners.  · 1913 to 1917: Welfare Workers` Association (WWA) · 1917 to 1924: Central Association of Welfare Workers (CAWW), Central Association of Welfare Workers (Industrial), Welfare Workers` Institute (WWI) · 1924 to 1931: Institute of Industrial Welfare Workers (IIWW) · 1931 to 1946: Institute of Labour Management (ILM) · 1946 to 1994: Institute of Personnel Management (IPM) · 1994 to 2000: Institute of Personnel and Development (IPD)- an amalgamation of the IPM and Institute of Training and Development (ITD) - (formerly Institute of Training Officers) · 2000 to present: Chartered Institute of Personnel and Development (CIPD)

Chartered status was achieved in 2000 and the CIPD came into existence from 1 July of that year

· CIPD professional qualifications

· Professional Assessment of Competence (PAC)

· Accreditation of Prior Certificated Learning (APCL)

· Affiliate membership

· Affiliate: a basic level of membership, not assessed against professional standards.

· Associate: awarded on completion of a support level certificate or relevant NVQ Level 3 and 4.

· Licentiate: awarded on completion of at least one of the first three fields of the Practitioner-level professional standards, and also on completion of relevant MBAs and NVQs (Level 5).

· Graduate: awarded on completion of all fields of the Practitioner-level professional standards, but where no significant HR experience is held.

· Chartered Member (Chartered MCIPD)
Awarded on request to graduate members with have three years` relevant managerial experience.

William Edwards Deming	William Edwards Deming was an American statistician, professor, author, lecturer, and consultant. Deming is widely credited with improving production in the United States during World War II, although he is perhaps best known for his work in Japan. There, from 1950 onward he taught top management how to improve design , product quality, testing and sales (the last through global markets) through various methods, including the application of statistical methods.

Chapter 8. Performance management and performance appraisal

Rhetoric	Rhetoric is the art of using language as a means to persuade. Along with grammar and logic or dialectic, Rhetoric is one of the three ancient arts of discourse. From ancient Greece to the late 19th Century, it was a central part of Western education, filling the need to train public speakers and writers to move audiences to action with arguments.
Job description	A Job description is a list of the general tasks, or functions, and responsibilities of a position. Typically, it also includes to whom the position reports, specifications such as the qualifications needed by the person in the job, salary range for the position, etc. A Job description is usually developed by conducting a job analysis, which includes examining the tasks and sequences of tasks necessary to perform the job.
Rating scale	A Rating scale is a set of categories designed to elicit information about a quantitative or a qualitative attribute. In the social sciences, common examples are the Likert scale and 1-10 Rating scales in which a person selects the number which is considered to reflect the perceived quality of a product.
	A Rating scale is an instrument that requires the rater to assign the rated object that have numerals assigned to them.
Organizational culture	Organizational culture is an idea in the field of Organizational studies and management which describes the psychology, attitudes, experiences, beliefs and values (personal and cultural values) of an organization. It has been defined as `the specific collection of values and norms that are shared by people and groups in an organization and that control the way they interact with each other and with stakeholders outside the organization.`
	This definition continues to explain organizational values, also known as `beliefs and ideas about what kinds of goals members of an organization should pursue and ideas about the appropriate kinds or standards of behavior organizational members should use to achieve these goals. From organizational values develop organizational norms, guidelines, or expectations that prescribe appropriate kinds of behavior by employees in particular situations and control the behavior of organizational members towards one another.`
	Organizational culture is not the same as corporate culture.

Chapter 9. Reward strategies in the tourism and hospitality Chapter 0 industry

Purchasing power	Purchasing power is the number of goods/services that can be purchased with a unit of currency. For example, if you had taken one dollar to a store in the 1950s, you would have been able to buy a greater number of items than you would today, indicating that you would have had a greater Purchasing power in the 1950s. Currency can be either a commodity money, like gold or silver, or fiat currency like US dollars.
Strategy	A strategy is a plan of action designed to achieve a particular goal. The word strategy has military connotations, because it derives from the Greek word for army. strategy is different from tactics.
Right	Rights are normative (e.g. legal, social, or ethical) principles of freedom or entitlement. That is to say, Rights are rules about what is allowed of people or owed to people, according to some legal system, social convention, or ethical theory. The concept of Rights is often fundamental to civilized societies, and it is of vital importance in such disciplines as law and ethics, especially theories of justice and deontology.
Job description	A Job description is a list of the general tasks, or functions, and responsibilities of a position. Typically, it also includes to whom the position reports, specifications such as the qualifications needed by the person in the job, salary range for the position, etc. A Job description is usually developed by conducting a job analysis, which includes examining the tasks and sequences of tasks necessary to perform the job.
Salary	A Salary is a form of periodic payment from an employer to an employee, which may be specified in an employment contract. It is contrasted with piece wages, where each job, hour or other unit is paid separately, rather than on a periodic basis. From the point of a business, Salary can also be viewed as the cost of acquiring human resources for running operations, and is then termed personnel expense or Salary expense.
Extreme value	The largest and the smallest element of a set are called extreme values, absolute extrema, extreme records, or optima. For a differentiable function f, if $f(x_0)$ is an extreme value for the set of all values $f(x)$, and if x_0 is in the interior of the domain of f, then x_0 is a critical point, by Fermat`s theorem. The point or points at which a function assumes its maximum (respectively, minimum) value are called the arg max (respectively, arg min): the arguments (inputs) at which the maximum (respectively, minimum) occurs.

Chapter 9. Reward strategies in the tourism and hospitality Chapter 0 industry

Minimum Wage	A Minimum wage is the lowest hourly, daily or monthly wage that employers may legally pay to employees or workers. Equivalently, it is the lowest wage at which workers may sell their labor. Although Minimum wage laws are in effect in a great many jurisdictions, there are differences of opinion about the benefits and drawbacks of a Minimum wage.
Motivation	Intrinsic Motivation has been studied by social and educational psychologists since the early 1970s. Research has found that it is usually associated with high educational achievement and enjoyment by students. Intrinsic Motivation has been explained by Fritz Heider`s attribution theory, Bandura`s work on self-efficacy, and Ryan and Deci`s cognitive evaluation theory. Students are likely to be intrinsically motivated if they:
	· attribute their educational results to internal factors that they can control ,
	· believe they can be effective agents in reaching desired goals (i.e. the results are not determined by luck),
	· are interested in mastering a topic, rather than just rote-learning to achieve good grades
	Extrinsic Motivation comes from outside of the performer.
McJob	McJob is slang for a low-paying, low-prestige job that requires few skills and offers very little chance of intracompany advancement. Such jobs are also known as contingent work. The term McJob comes from the name of the fast-food restaurant McDonald`s, but is used to describe any low-status job -- regardless of the employer -- where little training is required, staff turnover is high, and workers` activities are tightly regulated by managers.
Change management	Change management is a structured approach to transitioning individuals, teams, and organizations from a current state to a desired future state. In project management, Change management refers to a project management process where changes to a project are formally introduced and approved..
	The field of Change management grew from the recognition that organizations are composed of people.

Chapter 9. Reward strategies in the tourism and hospitality Chapter 0 industry

Remuneration	Remuneration is wages or salary, typically money that is paid for services rendered as an employee.
	Remuneration can include:
	· Commission
	· Compensation
	· Executive compensation
	· Deferred compensation
	· Compensation methods (in online advertising and internet marketing)
	· Employee stock option
	· Fringe benefit
	· Salary
	· Performance Linked Incentives
	· Wage
	·

Chapter 9. Reward strategies in the tourism and hospitality Chapter 0 industry

Travel agency	A travel agency is a retail business, that sells travel related products and services to customers, on behalf of suppliers, such as airlines, car rentals, cruise lines, hotels, railways, sightseeing tours and package holidays that combine several products. In addition to dealing with ordinary tourists, most travel agencies have a separate department devoted to making travel arrangements for business travelers and some travel agencies specialize in commercial and business travel only. There are also travel agencies that serve as general sales agents for foreign travel companies, allowing them to have offices in countries other than where their headquarters are located.
Wage	A Wage is a compensation, usually financial, received by workers in exchange for their labor. Compensation in terms of Wages is given to workers and compensation in terms of salary is given to employees. Compensation is a monetary benefit given to employees in return for the services provided by them.
Wage regulation	Wage regulation refers to attempts by a government to regulate wages paid to citizens. Minimum Wage regulation attempts to set an hourly, or other periodic monetary standard for pay at work. A recent example was the U.K. National Minimum Wage Act 1998. Germany is currently debating whether to introduce its own.
Commission	The Health and Safety Commission (HSC), was a United Kingdom non-departmental public body. The HSC was created by the Health and Safety at Work etc. Act 1974 (HSWA).
Apprenticeship	Apprenticeship is a system of training a new generation of practitioners of a skill. Apprentices or protégés build their careers from Apprenticeships. Most of their training is done on the job while working for an employer who helps the apprentices learn their trade, in exchange for their continuing labour for an agreed period after they become skilled.
Living wage	Living wage is a term used to describe the minimum hourly wage necessary for shelter (housing and incidentals such as clothing and other basic needs) and nutrition for a person for an extended period of time (lifetime). In developed countries such as the United Kingdom or Switzerland, this standard generally means that a person working forty hours a week, with no additional income, should be able to afford a specified quality or quantity of housing, food, utilities, transport, health care, and recreation.

This concept differs from the minimum wage in that the latter is set by law and may fail to meet the requirements of a Living wage.

Research

Research is defined as human activity based on intellectual application in the investigation of matter. The primary purpose for applied research is discovering, interpreting, and the development of methods and systems for the advancement of human knowledge on a wide variety of scientific matters of our world and the universe. research can use the scientific method, but need not do so.

Agenda

An agenda is a list of meeting activities in the order in which they are to be taken up, beginning with the call to order and ending with adjournment. It usually includes one or more specific items of business to be considered. It may, but is not required to, include specific times for one or more activities.

Chapter 10. Employee relations, involvement and participation

Industrial relations	Industrial relations is a multidisciplinary field that studies the employment relationship. Industrial relations is increasingly being called employment relations because of the importance of non-industrial employment relationships. Many outsiders also equate Industrial relations to labour relations and believe that Industrial relations only studies unionized employment situations, but this is an oversimplification. Industrial relations has three faces: science building, problem solving, and ethical. In the science building face, Industrial relations is part of the social sciences, and it seeks to understand the employment relationship and its institutions through high-quality, rigorous research. In this vein, Industrial relations scholarship intersects with scholarship in labor economics, industrial sociology, labor and social history, human resource management, political science, law, and other areas.
Chartered Institute of Personnel and Development	The Chartered Institute of Personnel and Development (CIPD) is Europe`s largest professional institute for people management and development. It is located in Wimbledon, London, England. The organisation has over 133,000 members, and achieved chartered status in 2000. The institute holds an annual conference for HR practitioners.   · 1913 to 1917: Welfare Workers` Association (WWA) · 1917 to 1924: Central Association of Welfare Workers (CAWW), Central Association of Welfare Workers (Industrial), Welfare Workers` Institute (WWI) · 1924 to 1931: Institute of Industrial Welfare Workers (IIWW) · 1931 to 1946: Institute of Labour Management (ILM) · 1946 to 1994: Institute of Personnel Management (IPM) · 1994 to 2000: Institute of Personnel and Development (IPD)- an amalgamation of the IPM and Institute of Training and Development (ITD) - (formerly Institute of Training Officers) · 2000 to present: Chartered Institute of Personnel and Development (CIPD) Chartered status was achieved in 2000 and the CIPD came into existence from 1 July of that year · CIPD professional qualifications

· Professional Assessment of Competence (PAC)

· Accreditation of Prior Certificated Learning (APCL)

· Affiliate membership

· Affiliate: a basic level of membership, not assessed against professional standards.

· Associate: awarded on completion of a support level certificate or relevant NVQ Level 3 and 4.

· Licentiate: awarded on completion of at least one of the first three fields of the Practitioner-level professional standards, and also on completion of relevant MBAs and NVQs (Level 5).

· Graduate: awarded on completion of all fields of the Practitioner-level professional standards, but where no significant HR experience is held.

· Chartered Member (Chartered MCIPD)
Awarded on request to graduate members with have three years` relevant managerial experience.

Conflict resolution	Conflict resolution is a range of methods for alleviating or eliminating sources of conflict. The term `Conflict resolution` is sometimes used interchangeably with the term dispute resolution or alternative dispute resolution. Processes of Conflict resolution generally include negotiation, mediation, and diplomacy.
Collective	A commune or intentional community, which may also be known as a `collective household`, is a group of people who live together in some kind of dwelling or residence, or in some other arrangement (eg. sharing land). collective households may be organized for a specific purpose .
Ethical bank	An Ethical bank is a bank concerned with the social and environmental impacts of its investments and loans. Ethical banks are part of a larger societal movement toward more social and environmental responsibility in the financial sector. This movement includes: ethical investment, socially responsible investment, corporate social responsibility, and is also related to such movements as the fair trade movement, ethical consumerism, boycotting, etc.

Chapter 10. Employee relations, involvement and participation

Partnership	Partnerships may be formed in the legal forms of General partnership (Offene Handelsgesellschaft, OHG) or Limited partnership (Kommanditgesellschaft, KG). A partnership can be formed by only one person. In the OHG, all partners are fully liable for the partnership`s debts, whereas in the KG there are general partners with unlimited liability and limited partners whose liability is restricted to their fixed contributions to the partnership.
Employment	Employment is a contract between two parties, one being the employer and the other being the employee. An employee may be defined as: `A person in the service of another under any contract of hire, express or implied, oral or written, where the employer has the power or right to control and direct the employee in the material details of how the work is to be performed.` Black`s Law Dictionary page 471 (5th ed. 1979). In a commercial setting, the employer conceives of a productive activity, generally with the intention of generating a profit, and the employee contributes labour to the enterprise, usually in return for payment of wages.
Employee Relations Act 1999	The Employee Relations Act 1999 is a British law. The Act allows workers to receive at least 3 months unpaid leave for the purpose of caring for a child. Mothers can have up to 18 weeks paid maternity leave.
Organization	An Organization is a social arrangement which pursues collective goals, controls its own performance, and has a boundary separating it from its environment. The word itself is derived from the Greek word organon, itself derived from the better-known word ergon. In the social sciences, Organizations are the object of analysis for a number of disciplines, such as sociology, economics, political science, psychology, management, and Organizational communication.
Two-way	Two-way communication occurs when information flows in both directions between two parties. In journalism, a two-way is an informal style of reporting that involves a conversation between two people. The most common arrangement is for a reporter in the field to talk to the host of a news program.
Two-way communication	Two-way communication - uses communication to negotiate with publics, resolve conflict, and promote mutual understanding and respect between the organization and its public(s).

Chapter 10. Employee relations, involvement and participation

Two-way communication in Public Relations

There are different types of Two-way communication in public relations; symmetric and asymmetric.

Two-way asymmetric public relations...

· can also be called `scientific persuasion;`

· employs social science methods to develop more ;

· generally focuses on achieving short-term attitude change;

· incorporates lots of feedback from target audiences and publics;

· is used by an organization primarily interested in having its publics come around to its way of thinking rather changing the organization, its policies, or its views.

Quality circle	A Quality circle is a volunteer group composed of workers (or even students), usually under the leadership of their supervisor (but they can elect a team leader), who are trained to identify, analyse and solve work-related problems and present their solutions to management in order to improve the performance of the organization, and motivate and enrich the work of employees. When matured, true Quality circles become self-managing, having gained the confidence of management. Quality circles are an alternative to the dehumanising concept of the division of labour, where workers or individuals are treated like robots.
Total quality management	Total quality management is a management concept coined by W. Edwards Deming. The basis of Total quality management is to reduce the errors produced during the manufacturing or service process, increase customer satisfaction, streamline supply chain management, aim for modernization of equipment and ensure workers have the highest level of training. One of the principal aims of Total quality management is to limit errors to 1 per 1 million units produced.

Chapter 10. Employee relations, involvement and participation

Job security	Job security is the probability that an individual will keep his or her job; a job with a high level of Job security is such that a person with the job would have a small chance of becoming unemployed. Job security is dependent on economy, prevailing business conditions, and the individual`s personal skills. It has been found that people have more Job security in times of economic expansion and less in times of a recession.
Works Council	A Works council is a `shop-floor` organization representing workers, which functions as local/firm-level complement to national labour negotiations. Works councils exist with different names in a variety of related forms in a number of European countries, including Germany and Austria , Luxembourg (Comité Mixte), the Netherlands and Flanders in Belgium (Ondernemingsraad), France (Comité d`Entreprise), Wallonia in Belgium (Conseil d`Entreprise), and Spain (Comité de empresa). One of the most commonly-examined (and arguably most successful) implementations of these institutions is found in Germany. The model is basically as follows: general labour agreements are made at the national level by national unions and national employer associations (e.g. Gesamtmetall), and local plants and firms then meet with Works councils to adjust these national agreements to local circumstances. Works council members are elected by the company workforce for a four year term. They don`t have to be union members; Works councils can also be formed in companies where neither the employer nor the employees are organized.
Regulations	The Control of Substances Hazardous to Health regulations 2002 is a United Kingdom Statutory Instrument that stipulates general requirements on employers to protect employees and other persons from the hazards of substances used at work by risk assessment, control of exposure, health surveillance and incident planning. There are also duties on employees to take care of their own exposure to hazardous substances and prohibitions on the import of certain substances into the European Economic Area. The regulations reenacted with amendements the Control of Substances Hazardous to Work regulations 1999 and implement several European Union directives.

Chapter 11. Welfare, health and safety

Conscience	Conscience is an ability or a faculty that distinguishes whether one`s actions are right or wrong. It leads to feelings of remorse when a human does things that go against his/her moral values, and to feelings of rectitude or integrity when actions conform to moral values. It is also often viewed as the attitude which informs moral judgment before an action is performed.
Equal	EQUAL was the `Community Initiative` within the European Social Fund of the European Union. It concerned `transnational co-operation to promote new means of combating all forms of discrimination and inEQUALities in connection with the labour market`. It ran from 2001 till 2007 with a budget of some â,¬3 billion of EU resources, matched by a similar sum from national resources.
Equality of opportunity	Equality of opportunity is a term which has differing definitions and there is no consensus as to the precise meaning. In the classical sense, Equality of opportunity is closely aligned with the concept of equality before the law, and ideas of meritocracy. Equality of opportunity is in philosophical contrast to the concept of equality of outcome.
Management	Management in all business areas and organizational activities are the acts of getting people together to accomplish desired goals and objectives. Management comprises planning, organizing, staffing, leading or directing, and controlling an organization or effort for the purpose of accomplishing a goal. Resourcing encompasses the deployment and manipulation of human resources, financial resources, technological resources, and natural resources.
Chartered Institute of Personnel and Development	The Chartered Institute of Personnel and Development (CIPD) is Europe`s largest professional institute for people management and development. It is located in Wimbledon, London, England. The organisation has over 133,000 members, and achieved chartered status in 2000. The institute holds an annual conference for HR practitioners.  · 1913 to 1917: Welfare Workers` Association (WWA) · 1917 to 1924: Central Association of Welfare Workers (CAWW), Central Association of Welfare Workers (Industrial), Welfare Workers` Institute (WWI) · 1924 to 1931: Institute of Industrial Welfare Workers (IIWW) · 1931 to 1946: Institute of Labour Management (ILM) · 1946 to 1994: Institute of Personnel Management (IPM) · 1994 to 2000: Institute of Personnel and Development (IPD)- an amalgamation of the IPM and Institute of Training and Development (ITD) - (formerly Institute of Training Officers)

· 2000 to present: Chartered Institute of Personnel and Development (CIPD)
Chartered status was achieved in 2000 and the CIPD came into existence from 1 July of that year

· CIPD professional qualifications

· Professional Assessment of Competence (PAC)

· Accreditation of Prior Certificated Learning (APCL)

· Affiliate membership

· Affiliate: a basic level of membership, not assessed against professional standards.

· Associate: awarded on completion of a support level certificate or relevant NVQ Level 3 and 4.

· Licentiate: awarded on completion of at least one of the first three fields of the Practitioner-level professional standards, and also on completion of relevant MBAs and NVQs (Level 5).

· Graduate: awarded on completion of all fields of the Practitioner-level professional standards, but where no significant HR experience is held.

· Chartered Member (Chartered MCIPD)
Awarded on request to graduate members with have three years` relevant managerial experience.

| Causality | Causality is the relationship between an event and a second event (the effect), where the second event is a direct consequence of the first.
The philosophical treatment of Causality extends over millennia. In the Western philosophical tradition, discussion stretches back at least to Aristotle, and the topic remains a staple in contemporary philosophy. |

Cram\101

Chapter 11. Welfare, health and safety

Organization	An Organization is a social arrangement which pursues collective goals, controls its own performance, and has a boundary separating it from its environment. The word itself is derived from the Greek word organon, itself derived from the better-known word ergon. In the social sciences, Organizations are the object of analysis for a number of disciplines, such as sociology, economics, political science, psychology, management, and Organizational communication.
Religious discrimination	Religious discrimination is valuing or treating a person or group differently because of what they do or do not believe. A concept like that of `Religious discrimination` is necessary to take into account ambiguities of the term religious persecution. The infamous cases in which people have been executed for beliefs perceived to be heretic are generally recognisable as persecution; Other cases in which adherents of different religions (or denominations) are treated unequally before the law are sometimes difficult to assess.
Bounded rationality	Bounded rationality is the notion that in decision making, rationality of individuals is limited by the information they have, the cognitive limitations of their minds, and the finite amount of time they have to make decisions. It was proposed by Herbert Simon as an alternative basis for the mathematical modeling of decision making, as used in economics and related disciplines; it complements rationality as optimization, which views decision making as a fully rational process of finding an optimal choice given the information available. Another way to look at Bounded rationality is that, because decision-makers lack the ability and resources to arrive at the optimal solution, they instead apply their rationality only after having greatly simplified the choices available.
Disability Discrimination Act	In the late 20th and early 21st centuries, a number of countries have passed laws aimed at reducing discrimination against people with disabilities. These laws have begun to appear as the notion of civil rights has become more influential globally, and follow other forms of anti-discrimination and equal opportunity legislation aimed at preventing racial discrimination and sexism which began to emerge in the second half of the 20th century. Australia Disability Discrimination Act 1992 Canada Ontarians with Disabilities Act (2002) (only in Ontario, no other province has disability protection) United Kingdom

Disability Discrimination Act 1995 (which has been extended and amended by a number of enactments including the Special Educational Needs and Disability Act 2001 , and the Disability Discrimination Act 2005)

United States of America
Americans with Disabilities Act of 1990

Pakistan
National Policy for Persons with Disablilities 2002

.

Consideration	Consideration is the legal concept of value in connection with contracts. It is anything of value in the common sense, promised to another when making a contract. It can take the form of money, physical objects, services, promised actions, or even abstinence from a future action.
Human Rights	Human rights are `basic rights and freedoms to which all humans are entitled.` Examples of rights and freedoms which have come to be commonly thought of as Human rights include civil and political rights, such as the right to life and liberty, freedom of expression, and equality before the law; and economic, social and cultural rights, including the right to participate in culture, the right to food, the right to work, and the right to education. Although other civilizations - notably those of Persia, India, China and the Islamic world - were at least equal to Europe at various stages in history, and in many respects in advance of it, they did not manage to propagate a universal ethics of rights. In the 16th century, the `Great Moghul,` Akbar the Great of India, granted religious minorities legal status in his realm and condemned traditional Indian practices such as the burning of widows (suttee) and slavery.
Human Rights Act	A Human Rights Act is a piece of legislation that sets out individual rights and freedoms under law. Many countries have similar rights enshrined into law; the countries with this naming convention tend to be Commonwealth countries. For specific variations see the articles for relevant act in the following countries: Australia

The ACT Human Rights Act 2004
The Victorian Charter of Human Rights and Responsibilities Act 2006

Canada

The Canadian Human Rights Act

New Zealand

The Human Rights Act 1993

United Kingdom

The Human Rights Act 1998

.

Human Rights Act 1998	The Human Rights Act 1998 is an Act of Parliament of the United Kingdom which received Royal Assent on 9 November 1998, and mostly came into force on 2 October 2000. Its aim is to `give further effect` in UK law to the rights contained in the European Convention on Human Rights. The Act makes available in UK courts a remedy for breach of a Convention right, without the need to go to the European Court of Human Rights in Strasbourg. It also totally abolished the death penalty in UK law (although this was not required by the Convention in force for the UK at that time).
Right	Rights are normative (e.g. legal, social, or ethical) principles of freedom or entitlement. That is to say, Rights are rules about what is allowed of people or owed to people, according to some legal system, social convention, or ethical theory. The concept of Rights is often fundamental to civilized societies, and it is of vital importance in such disciplines as law and ethics, especially theories of justice and deontology.
Sexual harassment	Sexual harassment is intimidation, bullying or coercion of a sexual nature, or the unwelcome or inappropriate promise of rewards in exchange for sexual favors. In some contexts or circumstances, Sexual harassment may be illegal. It includes a range of behavior from seemingly mild transgressions and annoyances to actual sexual abuse or sexual assault.
Cabin crew	Cabin crew (also known as Aviators, RobKAY [Rob Kittler] and - Ben Garden and others) are a Sydney duo of Ben Garden and Rob Kittler from Australia. They are best-known for their song, `Star To Fall` (also known as `Star2Fall`), which is a remix of the 1988 hit song `Waiting For A Star To Fall` by Boy Meets Girl, and was involved in a `sample battle` with Sunset Strippers. cabin crew originally remixed the track, but SonyBMG would not clear the sample for release.

Chapter 11. Welfare, health and safety

Brain drain	Brain drain or human capital flight is a large emigration of individuals with technical skills or knowledge, normally due to conflict, lack of opportunity, political instability, since emigrants usually take with them the fraction of value of their training sponsored by the government. It is a parallel of capital flight which refers to the same movement of financial capital.
Health and Safety Executive	The Health and Safety Executive is a non-departmental public body in the United Kingdom. It is the body responsible for the encouragement, regulation and enforcement of workplace health, safety and welfare, and for research into occupational risks in England and Wales and Scotland. Responsibility in Northern Ireland lies with the Health and Safety Executive for Northern Ireland.
Ethical bank	An Ethical bank is a bank concerned with the social and environmental impacts of its investments and loans. Ethical banks are part of a larger societal movement toward more social and environmental responsibility in the financial sector. This movement includes: ethical investment, socially responsible investment, corporate social responsibility, and is also related to such movements as the fair trade movement, ethical consumerism, boycotting, etc.
Role	A Role or a social Role is a set of connected behaviors, rights and obligations as conceptualized by actors in a social situation. It is an expected or free or continuously changing behavior and may have a given individual social status or social position. It is vital to both functionalist and interactionist understandings of society. Social Role posits the following about social behavior: · The division of labor in society takes the form of the interaction among heterogeneous specialized positions, we call Roles. · Social Roles included appropriate and permitted forms of behavior, guided by social norms, which are commonly known and hence determine the expectations for appropriate behavior in these Roles. · Roles are occupied by individuals, who are called actors. · When individuals approve of a social Role they will incur costs to conform to Role norms, and will also incur costs to punish those who violate Role norms. · Changed conditions can render a social Role outdated or illegitimate, in which case social pressures are likely to lead to Role change · The anticipation of rewards and punishments, as well as the satisfaction of behaving prosocially, account for why agents conform to Role requirements.

Chapter 11. Welfare, health and safety

Working time	Working time is the period of time that an individual spends at paid occupational labor. Unpaid labors such as personal housework are not considered part of the working week. Many countries regulate the work week by law, such as stipulating minimum daily rest periods, annual holidays and a maximum number of working hours per week.
Air rage	Air rage is the general term for disruptive and/or violent behavior perpetrated by passengers and crew of aircraft, typically during flight.
	Unlike ground vehicles, airplanes enter altitudes where changes in air pressure can help trigger temporary psychological changes, such as enhancing the psychoactive effects of chemicals like alcohol which is typically served on board.
	Furthermore, stopping and ejecting the offenders is often not a practical option as landing is an involved process that would seriously inconvenience the flight schedule of the aircraft and the passengers more than the misbehaving person themselves.
Workplace violence	Workplace violence refers to violence that originates from employees or employers and threatens employers and/or other employees.
	The definition of work related violence that has received pan-European acceptance is as follows:
	`incidents where people are abused, threatened or assaulted in circumstances relating to their work, involving an explicit or implicit challenge to their safety, well-being or health`.
	This can involve violence resulting from industrial disputes, although this is not a major factor in most incidents.

Chapter 12. Grievance and disciplinary procedures

ACAS	The Advisory, Conciliation and Arbitration Service (Acas) is a Crown non-departmental public body of the Government of the United Kingdom. Its purpose is to improve organisations and working life through the promotion and facilitation of strong industrial relations practice. It may do this through a number of mediums such as arbitration or mediation, although the service is perhaps best known for its collective conciliation function - that is resolving disputes between groups of employees or workers, often represented by a trade union, and their employers.
Arbitration	Arbitration, a form of alternative dispute resolution (ADR), is a legal technique for the resolution of disputes outside the courts, wherein the parties to a dispute refer it to one or more persons (the `arbitrators`, `arbiters` or `arbitral tribunal`), by whose decision (the `award`) they agree to be bound. It is a settlement technique in which a third party reviews the case and imposes a decision that is legally binding for both sides. Other forms of ADR include mediation and non-binding resolution by experts.
Chartered Institute of Personnel and Development	The Chartered Institute of Personnel and Development (CIPD) is Europe`s largest professional institute for people management and development. It is located in Wimbledon, London, England. The organisation has over 133,000 members, and achieved chartered status in 2000. The institute holds an annual conference for HR practitioners.    · 1913 to 1917: Welfare Workers` Association (WWA) · 1917 to 1924: Central Association of Welfare Workers (CAWW), Central Association of Welfare Workers (Industrial), Welfare Workers` Institute (WWI) · 1924 to 1931: Institute of Industrial Welfare Workers (IIWW) · 1931 to 1946: Institute of Labour Management (ILM) · 1946 to 1994: Institute of Personnel Management (IPM) · 1994 to 2000: Institute of Personnel and Development (IPD)- an amalgamation of the IPM and Institute of Training and Development (ITD) - (formerly Institute of Training Officers) · 2000 to present: Chartered Institute of Personnel and Development (CIPD) Chartered status was achieved in 2000 and the CIPD came into existence from 1 July of that year

· CIPD professional qualifications

· Professional Assessment of Competence (PAC)

· Accreditation of Prior Certificated Learning (APCL)

· Affiliate membership

· Affiliate: a basic level of membership, not assessed against professional standards.

· Associate: awarded on completion of a support level certificate or relevant NVQ Level 3 and 4.

· Licentiate: awarded on completion of at least one of the first three fields of the Practitioner-level professional standards, and also on completion of relevant MBAs and NVQs (Level 5).

· Graduate: awarded on completion of all fields of the Practitioner-level professional standards, but where no significant HR experience is held.

· Chartered Member (Chartered MCIPD)
Awarded on request to graduate members with have three years` relevant managerial experience.

Conciliation	Conciliation is an alternative dispute resolution (ADR) process whereby the parties to a dispute (including future interest disputes) agree to utilize the services of a conciliator, who then meets with the parties separately in an attempt to resolve their differences. He does this by lowering tensions, improving communications, interpreting issues, providing technical assistance, exploring potential solutions and bringing about a negotiated settlement. Conciliation differs from arbitration in that the Conciliation process, in and of itself, has no legal standing, and the conciliator usually has no authority to seek evidence or call witnesses, usually writes no decision, and makes no award.

Chapter 12. Grievance and disciplinary procedures

Employment	Employment is a contract between two parties, one being the employer and the other being the employee. An employee may be defined as: `A person in the service of another under any contract of hire, express or implied, oral or written, where the employer has the power or right to control and direct the employee in the material details of how the work is to be performed.` Black`s Law Dictionary page 471 (5th ed. 1979).
	In a commercial setting, the employer conceives of a productive activity, generally with the intention of generating a profit, and the employee contributes labour to the enterprise, usually in return for payment of wages.
Discipline	In its most general sense, Discipline refers to systematic instruction given to a disciple. To Discipline thus means to instruct a person to follow a particular code of conduct `order.` Usually, the phrase `to Discipline` carries a negative connotation. This is because enforcement of order - that is, ensuring instructions are carried out - is often regulated through punishment.
Contentment	Contentment is the experience of satisfaction and being at ease in one`s situation. Some of the earliest references to the state of Contentment are found in the reference to the midah (personal attribute) of Samayach B`Chelko. The expression comes from the word samayach (root Sin-Mem-Chet) meaning `happiness, joy `, and chelko (root Chet-Lamed-Kuf) meaning `portion, lot, or piece`, and combined mean Contentment with one`s lot in life.
Ethical bank	An Ethical bank is a bank concerned with the social and environmental impacts of its investments and loans. Ethical banks are part of a larger societal movement toward more social and environmental responsibility in the financial sector. This movement includes: ethical investment, socially responsible investment, corporate social responsibility, and is also related to such movements as the fair trade movement, ethical consumerism, boycotting, etc.
Degrees	· Degree symbol, (°), a notation used in science, engineering and mathematics
	· Degree (angle), a unit of angle measurement
	· Degree (temperature), a unit of temperature measurement
	· Degree API, a measure of density in the petroleum industry
	· Degree Baumé, a pair of density scales
	· Degree Brix, a measure of sugar concentration

Chapter 12. Grievance and disciplinary procedures

· Degree Gay-Lussac, a measure of the alcohol content of a liquid by volume, ranging from 0° to 100°

· Degree proof, or simply proof, the alcohol content of a liquid, ranging from 0° to 175° in the UK, and from 0° to 200° in the U.S.

· Degree of curvature, a unit of curvature measurement, used in civil engineering

· degrees of freedom (mechanics), the number of displacements and/or rotations needed to define the position and orientation of a body

· degrees of freedom (physics and chemistry), a concept describing dependence on a countable set of parameters

· Degree of frost, a unit of temperature measurement

· Degree of unsaturation, in organic chemistry, also known as the index of hydrogen deficiency or rings plus double bonds

· dGH, degrees of general hardness of water

· Degree of carbonate hardness of water (degree KH)

· Degree (mathematics), with several meanings

· Degree of a polynomial, the exponent of the term with the highest exponent

· Degree of a field extension

· Degree (graph theory), or valency, the number of edges incident to a vertex of a graph

· Degree of a continuous mapping

· degrees of freedom (statistics), the number of values in the final calculation of a statistic that are free to vary

· Academic degree, an academic award or title, including:

· Foundation degree

· Associate`s degree

· Bachelor`s degree

· Master`s degree

· Doctorate

· Engineer`s degree

· Specialist degree

· Ad eundem degree

· Honorary degree

· Lambeth degree

· External degree

· Vocational degree, an award in vocational education

· Degree (music), identification of a note in a scale by its relation to the tonic

· Degree of inventiveness in inventions and patents

· Degree of separation in connectivity between groups

· The positive, comparative, and superlative degrees, in linguistics (e.g. `good`, `better`, and `best`, respectively)

· Consanguinity, or level of kinship

· The severity of a crime, e.g., first degree murder

· The intensity of a burn, ranging from first degree to third degree

· A level of initiation, often used in fraternal organizations

· A ranking of black belt, in certain martial arts

· Degree (deodorant), a brand of antiperspirant

:

·

Employee Relations Act 1999	The Employee Relations Act 1999 is a British law. The Act allows workers to receive at least 3 months unpaid leave for the purpose of caring for a child. Mothers can have up to 18 weeks paid maternity leave.
Mandatory retirement	Mandatory retirement is the age at which persons who hold certain jobs or offices are required by statute to step down, or retire. Typically, Mandatory retirement is justified by the argument that certain occupations are either too dangerous or require high levels of physical and mental skill . However, since the age at which retirement is mandated is often somewhat arbitrary and not based upon an actual physical evaluation of an individual person, many view the practice as a form of age discrimination, or ageism.
Regulations	The Control of Substances Hazardous to Health regulations 2002 is a United Kingdom Statutory Instrument that stipulates general requirements on employers to protect employees and other persons from the hazards of substances used at work by risk assessment, control of exposure, health surveillance and incident planning. There are also duties on employees to take care of their own exposure to hazardous substances and prohibitions on the import of certain substances into the European Economic Area. The regulations reenacted with amendements the Control of Substances Hazardous to Work regulations 1999 and implement several European Union directives.

CVam101

Chapter 12. Grievance and disciplinary procedures

Right	Rights are normative (e.g. legal, social, or ethical) principles of freedom or entitlement. That is to say, Rights are rules about what is allowed of people or owed to people, according to some legal system, social convention, or ethical theory. The concept of Rights is often fundamental to civilized societies, and it is of vital importance in such disciplines as law and ethics, especially theories of justice and deontology.
Employment tribunal	Employment Tribunals are tribunal non-departmental public bodies in England and Wales and Scotland which have statutory jurisdiction to hear many kinds of disputes between employers and employees. The most common disputes are concerned with unfair dismissal, redundancy payments and employment discrimination. The Tribunals are part of the UK tribunals system, administered by the Tribunals Service and regulated and supervised by the Administrative Justice and Tribunals Council.

Chapter 13. Concluding comments

Best practice	A Best practice is a technique, method, process, activity, incentive, or reward that is believed to be more effective at delivering a particular outcome than any other technique, method, process, etc. when applied to a particular condition or circumstance. The idea is that with proper processes, checks, and testing, a desired outcome can be delivered with fewer problems and unforeseen complications.

Lightning Source UK Ltd.
Milton Keynes UK
UKOW01f0501200214

226821UK00004B/125/P